AR PTS: 0.5

SPOTLIGHT ON
IMMIGRATION AND MIGRATION

THE CALIFORNIA GOLD RUSH

CHINESE LABORERS IN AMERICA (1848–1882)

Steve Wilson

PowerKiDS press.

NEW YORK

Published in 2016 by The Rosen Publishing Group, Inc.
29 East 21st Street, New York, NY 10010

Copyright © 2016 by The Rosen Publishing Group, Inc.

Editor: Sarah Machajewski
Book Design: Samantha DeMartin

Photo Credits: Cover, p. 10 Hulton Archive/Archive Photos/Getty Images; pp. 4, 5, 7, 12–13 Courtesy of the Library of Congress; p. 8 The Bancroft Library, University of California, Berkeley/Wikimedia Commons; p. 9 Alinari Archives/Alinari/Getty Images; pp. 11, 15 Everett Historical/Shutterstock.com; p. 17 Andrey Bayda/Shutterstock.com; p. 19 Museum of Chinese in America/Wikimedia Commons; p. 21 UniversalImagesGroup/Universal Images Group/Getty Images; p. 22 Monkey Business Images/Shutterstock.com.

Library of Congress Cataloging-in-Publication Data

Wilson, Steve, 1943-
The California gold rush : Chinese laborers in America (1848-1882) / Steve Wilson.
    pages cm. — (Spotlight on immigration and migration)
 Includes index.
ISBN 978-1-5081-4061-0 (pbk.)
ISBN 978-1-5081-4062-7 (6 pack)
ISBN 978-1-5081-4064-1 (library binding)
1. Chinese—United States—History—19th century—Juvenile literature. 2. Chinese Americans—United States—History—19th century—Juvenile literature. I. Title.
 E184.C5W56 2016
 973'.04951—dc23
                                    2015022273

Manufactured in the United States of America

CPSIA Compliance Information: Batch #BW16PK: For further information contact Rosen Publishing, New York, New York at 1-800-237-9932.

CONTENTS

THE LURE OF GOLD

The California gold rush began in 1848. About 300,000 gold seekers traveled to California after learning gold was found at a mill near Sacramento. People of all backgrounds were drawn to the territory, including Chinese **immigrants**. Before the gold rush, there were very few Chinese in America. By 1852, about 25,000 Chinese had come to find their fortune in the West. Even after the gold rush, the Chinese kept coming in large numbers. They came to escape a life of **poverty** in China.

Chinese immigrants are shown arriving in San Francisco, California, in this 1877 wood engraving. Customs officers, or officers who worked in immigration offices, check the immigrants' bags.

Chinese immigrants worked hard in all kinds of jobs, and they played a huge role in developing the American West. Despite this, many American citizens **discriminated** against them. In 1882, a U.S. law banned immigration to America from China. This law lasted until 1943.

SAN FRANCISCO HARBOR, 1850

HOW THE GOLD RUSH BEGAN

The California gold rush began with a man named John Sutter. Sutter was a German immigrant. He came to California in 1839. He founded a fort, which became very successful. The rest of his family followed a few years later. Sutter began building a sawmill in 1847 in Coloma, California, near the American River. In January 1848, James Marshall, one of Sutter's crew members who was working on the mill, found gold flakes in the river.

At first, Sutter tried to keep the discovery a secret. He didn't want large numbers of people coming to look for gold. However, it wasn't long before word got out. Word often reached other countries before it made its way to the eastern United States. Soon, people started coming to California from all parts of the world. One place from which many gold seekers came was China.

Jim Marshall stands in front of Sutter's sawmill, where he discovered gold.

CHASING OPPORTUNITY

The discovery of gold in California was an exciting time for America. However, on the other side of the world, China's people were suffering great hardship and poverty. High taxes after a war with England forced many peasants and farmers off their land. Then, years of flooding followed by long dry spells made matters worse.

In China, the average family depended on farming to make a living. Many farmers couldn't grow enough food on their small pieces of land to feed their growing families. When word of the gold in California reached China, many farmers began sending their sons to America. If all went according to plan, the sons could send money back to China to help their families.

Many Chinese lived in poverty. This photograph, which was taken in the late 1800s, shows Chinese men without shoes and in tattered clothing.

"GOLD MOUNTAIN"

The thought of gold was enough to draw the Chinese to California. Chinese ship owners played a part in encouraging **emigration** to America, too. They could make a lot of money by taking passengers there, so they printed advertisements that told of great wealth. The advertisements said the wealth could be found at *Gam Saan*, which means "Gold Mountain" in the Chinese language of Cantonese.

Many Chinese couldn't pay for the passage to America. Chinese merchants lent people money for their journey. Some immigrants paid their money back, with interest, from their earnings in America. Interest was an extra payment on top of the money that was borrowed. Others worked directly for the merchants when they arrived in their new home. Many Chinese found work in mining and other industries.

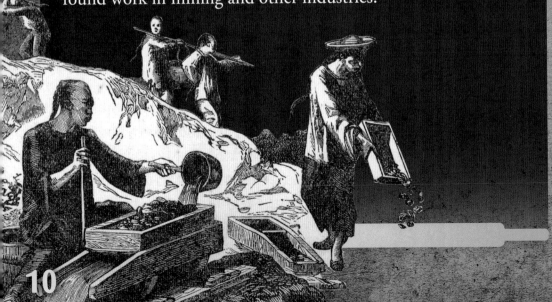

Chinese workers use this box, which is called a sluice, to control the flow of water from a nearby stream. They're using the stream's water to wash gold out of dirt and stone.

SAN FRANCISCO, THE PORT CITY

Some Chinese immigrants arrived in America in 1848, but the large waves of immigration started in the 1850s. Most of the Chinese immigrants sailed out of the port city Guangzhou, which is on the southeast coast of China.

The journey to California wasn't easy. Immigrants sailed on small, crowded ships and slept below the deck on bunks packed tightly together. The ships also carried goods that were to be sold in California, such as tea, silk, and certain kinds of fruit. These things weren't easy to get in California and sold well once they arrived there.

The voyage from China to America usually took eight weeks. The **destination** was San Francisco. San Francisco wasn't far from where gold was discovered.

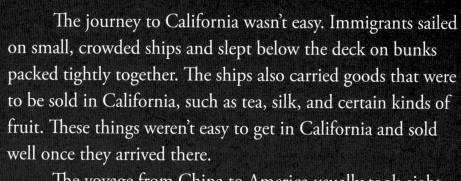

This image is an artist's view of San Francisco in its early days. Several figures along the bottom of the artwork are likely Chinese.

SETTING UP CAMP

Upon arriving in San Francisco, Chinese immigrants got straight to work. Their goal was to find gold. They set up mining camps by rivers and streams. Usually keeping to themselves, the Chinese miners lived in tents.

The Chinese faced many difficulties. By the time most of them arrived in California, the easily found gold had already been discovered. People who arrived in the years after the first rush learned that finding gold was now more difficult. Chinese miners worked hard, spending long hours in all kinds of weather, sifting sand from the riverbeds. Unfortunately, they rarely found gold settled at the bottom of their pan. Later, gold had to be mined from the mountains, which was even harder work. Over time, it became clear to many that they weren't going to get rich from finding gold.

This illustration shows Chinese miners and their camp, which was likely established along a river.

CHINATOWN GROWS

The California gold rush only lasted a short time. It was over by the mid-1850s. Large companies took over the task of gold mining. Chinese immigrants had a choice: they could either take jobs with these companies, or they could find work elsewhere. Most of them found other jobs.

The Chinese immigrants were willing to work long hours for low pay because they needed to send money to their families in China. Some immigrants cooked in restaurants. Others opened shops. One popular business was **laundry**. At this time, American men didn't do their own laundry. They felt it was a woman's job. There were few women in San Francisco—it was a **frontier** town settled by men. This created an opportunity for the Chinese to have successful laundry businesses.

Many Chinese settled in San Francisco after the gold rush ended. A large Chinese neighborhood grew and came to be known as Chinatown. Today, it's still a thriving neighborhood.

ANTI-CHINESE FEELINGS GROW

When the gold rush began, Americans in search of gold (who were called "forty-niners") didn't mind sharing their good fortune with the Chinese. It seemed that there was plenty of gold to go around. However, that feeling didn't last long. As more immigrants arrived in California and gold became harder to find, competition for the shiny metal increased. American miners who hadn't found gold grew **frustrated** and took their anger out on many immigrants, especially the Chinese. During this time, the Chinese faced increased discrimination.

In 1850, the California government passed the Foreign Miners Tax, which required each foreign miner to pay $20 per month to the state of California. That's equal to $625 today! Some Chinese paid the tax and continued searching for gold. Others felt that there wasn't enough gold available to make paying the tax worthwhile.

Riots in major western cities, such as Los Angeles and Denver, resulted in violence and sometimes death against these cities' Chinese residents.

BUILDING THE RAILROADS

Although the gold rush hadn't fulfilled its promises, Chinese immigrants continued arriving in America. Like those who had come before, these immigrants came looking for work. Many found jobs building the Central Pacific Railroad. The railroad started in California and continued east over the Sierra Nevada. In 1869, the railroad was connected with the Union Pacific Railroad at Promontory Summit, Utah. This was the first railroad that crossed the United States.

The Chinese immigrants worked hard to build the railroad. They became known for their good **work ethic**, even though the work was dangerous. Chinese workers placed the **dynamite** used to blast through rock in the mountains, and many died from accidents. In spite of their hard work, they were paid less than Americans who worked alongside them.

In 1868, Chinese laborers made up 80 percent of the Central Pacific workforce.

WITHSTANDING HARDSHIP

An economic **depression** in the late 1870s left many Californians out of work. Once again, they took their anger out on the Chinese. They accused the Chinese of taking their jobs. In 1882, the United States Congress passed the Chinese Exclusion Act, which banned immigration from China. The law lasted for 61 years, until 1943.

When the Chinese first left their homeland, it was to escape hardship. However, once they arrived in America, they discovered a different kind of hardship. Hardworking and patient, these Chinese immigrants still managed to make a decent life for themselves. After many years, Americans are finally starting to recognize the important contributions these immigrants made—and are still making—to the history of our country.

GLOSSARY

depression: A long period of economic troubles.

destination: The place to which someone or something is going.

discriminate: To unfairly treat people unequally.

dynamite: A powerful explosive.

emigration: The act of leaving one's country in order to settle in another.

frontier: Having to do with part of a country that has been newly opened for settlement.

frustrated: Feeling angry because of the inability to do something.

immigrant: A person who comes to live permanently in a new country.

laundry: A place where clothes are washed.

poverty: The state of being extremely poor.

work ethic: The belief that it is good to work hard.

INDEX

PRIMARY SOURCE LIST

Page 4. Chinese immigrants at the San Francisco custom-house. Created by P. Frenzeny. Wood engraving. Featured on the cover of *Harper's Weekly* on February 3, 1877. Now kept at the Library of Congress Prints and Photographs Division, Washington, D.C.

Page 7. Chinese Emigration to America: Sketch on board the Pacific Mail Steamship Alaska. Creator unknown. Published in *The Illustrated London News*, *The Graphic*, and *Harper's Weekly*. April 29, 1876. Now kept at the University of California, Berkeley, Bancroft Library, Berkeley, California.

Pages 12–13. View from Hilltop of San Francisco. Created by Frank Marryat. Chromolithograph. ca. 1850. Now kept at the Library of Congress Prints and Photographs Division, Washington, D.C.

WEBSITES

Due to the changing nature of Internet links, PowerKids Press has developed an online list of websites related to the subject of this book. This site is updated regularly. Please use this link to access the list: www.powerkidslinks.com/soim/chin